Scary Creatures of the ARCTIC

Written by
Penny Clarke

FRANKLIN WATTS
An Imprint of Scholastic Inc.
NEW YORK • TORONTO • LONDON • AUCKLAND • SYDNEY
MEXICO CITY • NEW DELHI • HONG KONG
DANBURY, CONNECTICUT

Created and designed
by David Salariya

Author:

Penny Clarke is an author and editor specializing in nonfiction books for children. She has written titles on natural history, rain forests, and volcanoes, as well as books on various periods in history. She used to live in central London, but thanks to modern technology she has now fulfilled her dream of being able to live and work in the countryside.

Artists:

John Francis
Robert Morton
Carolyn Scrace
Mark Bergin
Richard Coombes
Bob Hersey

Series Creator:

David Salariya was born in Dundee, Scotland. In 1989 he established The Salariya Book Company. He has illustrated a wide range of books and has created many new series for publishers in the U.K. and overseas. He lives in Brighton, England, with his wife, illustrator Shirley Willis, and their son.

Editor: Stephen Haynes

Editorial Assistants:
Rob Walker, Tanya Kant

Picture Research:
Mark Bergin, Carolyn Franklin

Created, designed, and produced by
The Salariya Book Company Ltd
Book House
25 Marlborough Place
Brighton BN1 1UB

A CIP catalog record for this title is available from the Library of Congress.

ISBN-13: 978-0-531-20449-8 (Lib. Bdg.)
978-0-531-21008-6 (Pbk.)
ISBN-10: 0-531-20449-9 (Lib. Bdg.)
0-531-21008-1 (Pbk.)

Published in the United States by Franklin Watts
An Imprint of Scholastic Inc.
557 Broadway
New York, NY 10012

Printed in China.

PAPER FROM
SUSTAINABLE
FORESTS

Photo Credits:

t=top, b=bottom, l=left, r=right

B. & C. Alexander/NHPA: 18, 24, 25
Tom Brakefield/Verve: 9t, 11, 28
Cadmium: 12r, 20, 26
Corbis: 4
Corel: 5b, 8, 10, 12l, 17, 19t, 29, 32
Digivis: 14, 27
John Foxx Images: 13
Mountain High Maps/©1993
  Digital Wisdom Inc.: 6–7
Photodisc: 5t, 9b, 19b

Polar bear

Contents

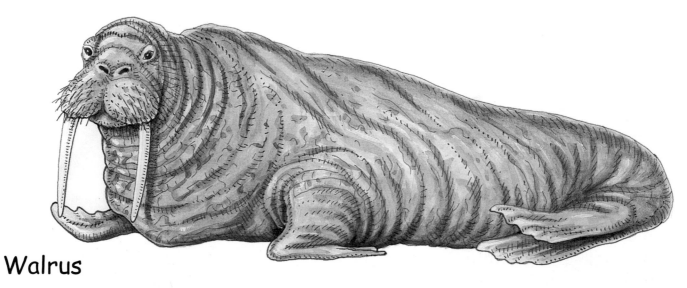

Walrus

What Is the Arctic?

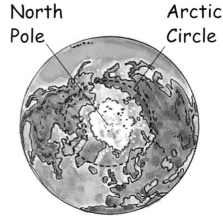

North Pole

Arctic Circle

To scientists, the Arctic is the area around the **North Pole**. But, in general, "Arctic" describes everywhere north of the **Arctic Circle**—the part of the world where the sun never rises in winter and never sets in summer.

The North Pole is the northern point of the **axis** around which the Earth **rotates**. The **South Pole** is its southern point.

Musk oxen form a protective group

Animals that live in the Arctic, like these musk oxen, must survive winters with temperatures many degrees below zero.

Did You Know?

Adult polar bears are more than 6.5 feet (2 m) long and weigh up to 1,500 pounds (700 kg). Despite their size, they can outrun humans and **reindeer**. They often stand by holes in the ice, waiting for seals to come up for air.

Polar bear

White fur is good **camouflage** on ice.

Some Arctic animals, such as Arctic foxes, have different coats in summer and winter. In winter they have thick white fur that camouflages them as they hunt along the snow-covered ground. When the snow melts in spring, they **molt** and grow brown fur again.

Arctic fox in winter

5

Where Is the Arctic?

Arctic animals

This map shows exactly where the Arctic is. Each of the Earth's northern landmasses has an Arctic region, with long, very cold winters and short, cool summers.

Much of the Arctic is **tundra**—land where the soil below the surface stays frozen all the time. Each spring the melting snow uncovers the tundra plants, which are eaten by such land animals as hares and lemmings. Most of the Antarctic has no tundra—and so no land animals.

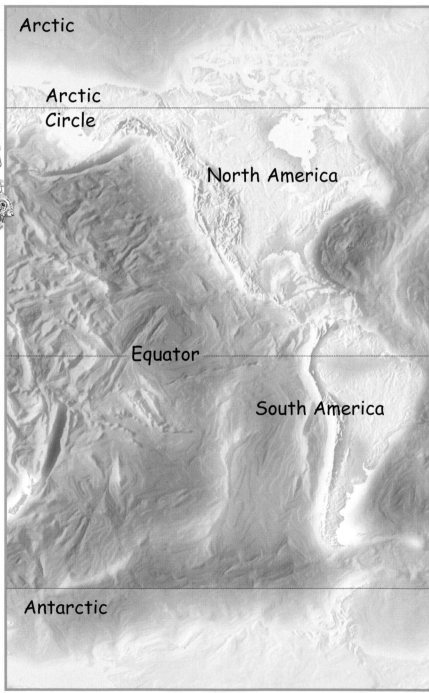

Arctic

Arctic Circle

North America

Equator

South America

Antarctic

"Antarctic" comes from a Greek word meaning "opposite to the north."

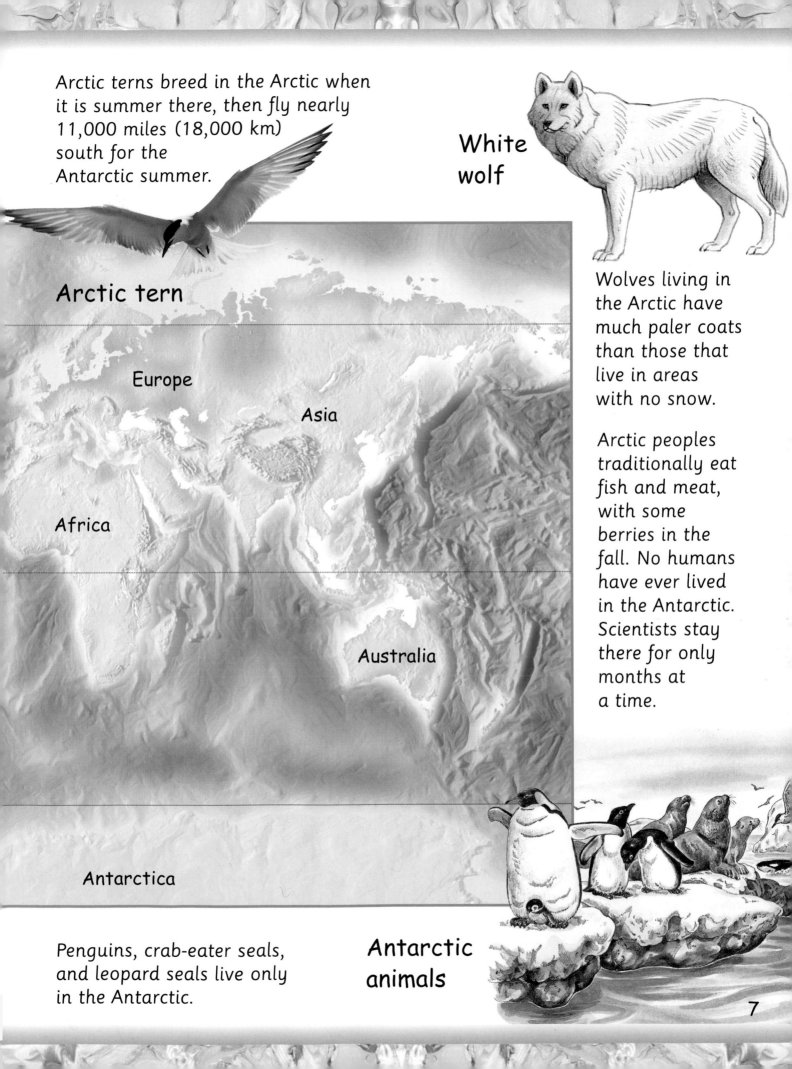

Arctic terns breed in the Arctic when it is summer there, then fly nearly 11,000 miles (18,000 km) south for the Antarctic summer.

Arctic tern

White wolf

Wolves living in the Arctic have much paler coats than those that live in areas with no snow.

Arctic peoples traditionally eat fish and meat, with some berries in the fall. No humans have ever lived in the Antarctic. Scientists stay there for only months at a time.

Europe

Asia

Africa

Australia

Antarctica

Penguins, crab-eater seals, and leopard seals live only in the Antarctic.

Antarctic animals

Are the Arctic and Antarctic Alike?

The climates of the Arctic and Antarctic are definitely alike. Both are cold and harsh, with brief summers and very long winters. But there are important differences between the two regions. The Arctic is a sheet of incredibly thick ice floating on a very, very cold sea. The Antarctic, however, is a landmass. Beneath its covering of snow and ice is rock that is part of the Earth's crust.

Why does a narwhal have a tusk?

No one knows why male narwhals have a tusk. The tusk (really an upper tooth) can be up to 9 feet (2.7 m) long.

Tusk

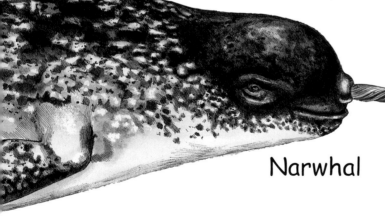

Narwhal

What is a wolverine?

Wolverines are related to weasels. Extremely strong, they can kill animals larger than themselves. They can also climb trees. Wolverines can be found in the forests at the edge of the Arctic.

Wolverine

Wolf

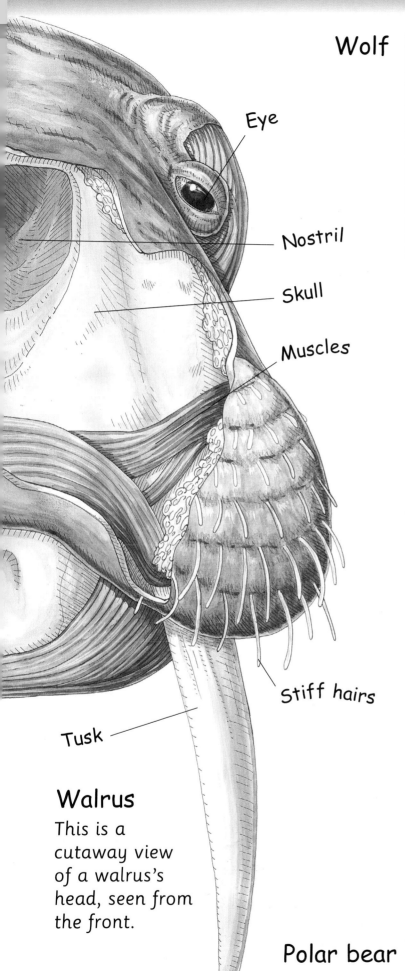

Eye

Nostril

Skull

Muscles

Stiff hairs

Tusk

Walrus

This is a cutaway view of a walrus's head, seen from the front.

Wolves usually hunt in packs, working as a team to catch **prey** like reindeer and elk. On their own, they also catch small animals such as mice. Both grey timber wolves and white Arctic wolves live in the Arctic Circle.

The walrus is another Arctic animal. Males have much larger tusks than females, but both have stiff whiskers.

Polar bears have dense coats to keep them warm as they swim between **ice floes** or hunt over the ice.

Polar bear

9

What Is the Arctic Climate Like?

Tough! Winter temperatures fall to about –22° Fahrenheit (–30° C) and the sun doesn't rise for months. Why? The Earth is tilted on its axis as it circles the sun. For half the year the northern part tilts away from the sun, causing the Arctic's winter. At the same time, the Earth's southern part is tilted toward the sun and the Antarctic has its summer.

Arctic hare

Birds and some mammals avoid Arctic winters by **migrating** south, but other animals live there all year. Arctic hares move from the open tundra to areas where there are more shrubs to shelter them. The hares' winter coats are white, camouflaging them from **predators**. They dig through the snow to reach the plants they eat.

Lemmings also have no problems with Arctic winters. They have white winter coats, but spend much of the time safely under the snow, searching for moss and other plants to eat. In spring, the females have their first **litters** of the year in burrows under the snow.

Lemming

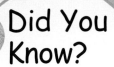

Did You Know?

Polar bear cubs stay with their mother for about two years. Then they move away to find their own territory.

Female polar bears make deep dens in the snow. There they give birth, usually to two cubs. The cubs stay in the den until the spring thaw begins. Then their mother leads them outside and starts teaching them to hunt.

Female polar bear with her cub

What Happens in the Winter?

To survive in the Arctic, living things have adapted in different ways. Some birds migrate south to warmer places hundreds or thousands of miles away. Others, like the ptarmigan, just move from the open tundra to the shelter of birch and conifer forests closer to the Arctic Circle. Like many arctic mammals, some birds look quite different in summer and winter.

Ptarmigans do not migrate very far. They spend summers on the open Arctic tundra and winters near the shelter of woods and forests. Their feathers match these **habitats**: speckled in summer to blend with plants and stones, and white in winter to match the snow.

Ptarmigan in summer plumage   Ptarmigan in winter plumage

Snowy owl

The snowy owl is one of the Arctic's great hunters. It likes rocky ground, where it perches on rocks to spot its prey of lemmings, voles, and rabbits.

Did You Know?

Only the adult males are really snowy white. Females have spots on their heads and bands on their wings. Young snowy owls have even more dark bands and spots—it takes a year before they look like their parents.

Is the North Pole Just Ice?

Yes! There is no land under the North Pole or the ice around it—just the Arctic Ocean. In 1958 the American submarine USS *Nautilus* proved this by sailing under the ice sheet to cross the Arctic Ocean.

X-Ray Vision

Hold the next page up to the light see one way that polar bears hunt.

See what's inside

Young polar bears
Play-fighting helps them develop their strength.

Do Plants Survive in the Arctic?

On the ice sheet itself, they don't. Closer to the Arctic Circle, plants survive by staying small. Large plants can't survive in the Arctic. Summers are too short, soils are too poor, and the wind would destroy them. Winter snow protects low-growing plants but can damage trees. Conifers have adapted by having branches that slope downward to throw off the snow.

Did You Know?

In spring, as the snow melts and plants start growing again, **caribou** herds move slowly north, grazing on the new growth. In winter they must dig through the snow for food.

Caribou (reindeer)

Can Anything Live in the Arctic Ocean?

Oh yes! These two pages show three animals that survive in the Arctic Ocean. The killer whale, or orca, is the only one that never comes onto land. Polar bears are really land animals that swim well. Seals spend most of their lives in the ocean, coming onto land to molt and have their young.

Harp seals

A thick layer of fatty **blubber** protects these harp seals from the cold of the Arctic Ocean. Baby harp seals have pure white fur.

On land, harp seals are slow and defenseless, but in the water their streamlined bodies make them fast and very agile swimmers.

Did You Know?

In the water, seals are too fast for polar bears. So the bears wait on the ice for the seals to come up for air. Then they kill them with one blow of their powerful forepaw.

Killer whales

Killer whales eat fish, squid, seals, and seabirds. They live in the Arctic and Antarctic oceans but do not migrate from one to the other.

Polar bear fishing

Polar bears have membranes of skin between their toes. These help them to swim well.

Do Scary Creatures Live in the Arctic?

If you were being chased by a polar bear, the answer would definitely be "Yes!" But although the tusks of these male walruses make them look very fierce, you may not be in any danger from them— they don't hunt humans.

Walruses

X-Ray Vision

Hold the page opposite up to the light and see what is inside a walrus!

See what's inside

Male walruses often fight each other for mates, and their tusks can cause severe wounds. The females also have tusks, but they are smaller than those of the males.

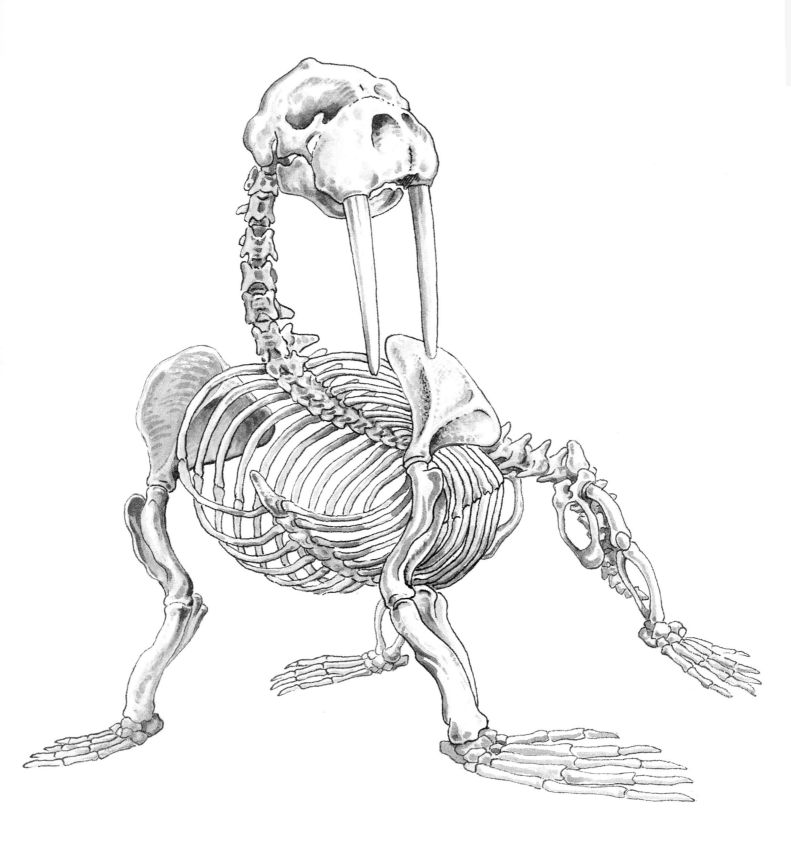

How Does a Walrus Hunt?

Walruses hunt underwater because they eat mainly shellfish and other creatures living on the seabed. They can stay submerged for up to ten minutes and dive to a depth of 100 feet (30 m). They eat only the soft parts of shellfish, probably sucking them out of the shell, although scientists are not sure how.

Getting onto the ice from the water is difficult for such heavy animals—males can weigh 3,000 pounds (1,361 kg). They can use their tusks—which are really two upper teeth—to haul themselves out of the ocean.

Once, walruses were hunted for the ivory in their tusks and nearly became **extinct**.

Walrus under the ice

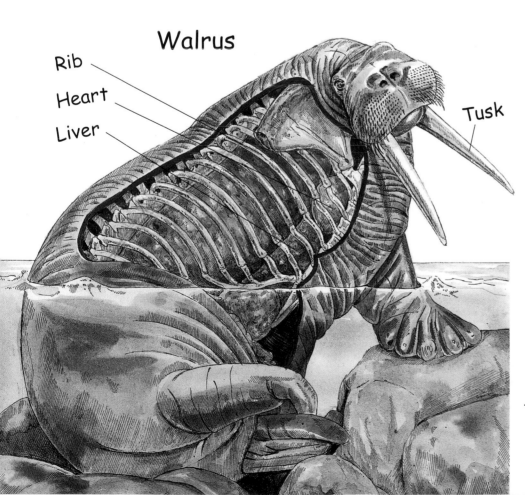

Walrus

Rib

Heart

Liver

Tusk

When not hunting, walruses live on the ice. They also used to live on beaches around the Arctic Ocean, but thousands were killed for their oily blubber and ivory. Now they stay away from places where humans live.

Do People Live in the Arctic?

Yes. Such peoples as the Inuit in Alaska and Canada, the Sami of Lapland, and the Chukchis of Siberia have all adapted to the Arctic's harsh conditions. They live as hunters and herders because the climate is too cold for growing crops.

Did You Know?

In winter at the North or the South poles the sun stays below the horizon for 186 days. This makes polar winters long, dark, and very cold.

Inuit driving dog sled

The Inuit of North America use sleds drawn by dog teams to travel over the Arctic's frozen ground.

Dogs are strong and their soft feet splay out, spreading their weight so they don't sink into the snow.

The Sami of Lapland (northern Scandinavia) are reindeer herders. In spring the herds move north to graze on the Arctic tundra. Then, when days shorten and temperatures start falling, they return south to more sheltered areas. These traditional clothes (below) are worn only on special occasions.

Sami reindeer herder

Inuit hunter

The Inuit often hunt through the ice (above). After diving, seals need to come to the surface for air. Knowing this, the Inuit make holes in the ice. When a seal's head appears above the ice, the waiting hunter traps and kills it.

25

Is the Arctic in Danger?

Yes, it is. Most scientists believe that the Earth's climate is heating up, with warmer winters and hotter summers. They call this "global warming." The North Pole is just an ice sheet, and ice melts if temperatures rise. This is already happening. And it's not just the ice sheet that's in danger; the whole Arctic region and the Arctic Ocean are, too.

Power stations burning **fossil fuels** give us energy, but also release gases that increase global warming.

Did You Know?

Polar bears need large hunting grounds. Scientists fear the bears will become extinct if the melting ice sheet gets too small for them.

Polar bear on an ice floe

How Can We Help?

Most of us will never visit the Arctic, but we can all help to preserve it for the future. How? By learning about global warming and how it affects the Earth. Most of the things we buy have been made in factories that use energy and cause pollution. Do we need all these things?

Baby harp seals are killed for their beautiful white fur—only the babies have pure white fur. Do we really need to wear furs for warmth? Or would it be better not to buy anything made of animal fur?

Harp seal pup

Each year, hundreds of baby seals are killed, supposedly to protect fish stocks. But what causes most damage to fish: seals, or huge fishing nets?

Grey wolves (timber wolves)

These grey wolves are taking a rest on the edge of a conifer forest.

Arctic Facts

The Arctic Ocean is the world's smallest ocean. It is also the shallowest, with an average depth of 3,248 feet (990 m). The Pacific, the largest and deepest ocean, has an average depth of 14,000 feet (4,280 m).

The Northwest Passage —a sea route linking the Atlantic and Pacific via the Arctic Ocean—is 3,200 miles (5,150 km) long, but that's much shorter than the route through the Panama Canal. The passage used to exist only in the brief Arctic summer, when sea ice melted. Even then, **icebergs** were a constant danger. But in summer 2007, the Northwest Passage was ice-free for the first time. This shocked scientists. They had expected this to happen, but not before about 2020.

If the Arctic continues to get warmer, ships might be able to sail across the Arctic Ocean, at least in summer.

Icebergs are huge masses of ice that have broken away from glaciers. Glaciers move very, very slowly downhill like rivers of ice. When they reach the sea, parts break off to form icebergs.

Icebergs are huge; some can be 1,500 feet (450 m) from top to bottom. But usually, only about a fifth of an iceberg shows above the water, giving us the saying "the tip of the iceberg."

Icebergs have sunk thousands of ships. The *Titanic*, which sank in 1912, is the best known; the ship's builders claimed it was "unsinkable."

Each summer, ice around the edge of the Arctic ice sheet melts. But in the fall, as temperatures drop, the ice re-forms.

The surface of the Arctic tundra thaws in the spring and summer, forming hundreds of boggy pools. The water in the pools cannot drain away because underneath is the **permafrost**—ground that never thaws. Huge clouds of insects hover over the pools, providing food for the many birds that spend the summer in the Arctic. Most of these birds nest on the ground. Why? There are no trees, because tree roots cannot grow into the frozen ground.

Polar bears

Glossary

Arctic Circle The latitude 66° 33' north of the Equator.

axis The imaginary line through the middle of the Earth around which the planet rotates.

blubber A thick, fatty layer under the skin of Arctic mammals such as whales and walruses. It helps protect them from the cold.

camouflage Markings or coloring on an animal that help it blend with its surroundings.

caribou A large species of Arctic deer; they are called caribou in North America and **reindeer** elsewhere.

extinct No longer alive anywhere on Earth.

fossil fuel A fuel, such as coal or gas, formed from the remains of living things that died millions of years ago.

habitat The natural environment in which a plant or animal lives.

iceberg A huge chunk of ice floating in the sea, but mostly underwater.

ice floe A huge, flat slab of floating ice.

litter A group of baby animals all born from the same mother at the same time.

migrate To leave a region at a particular time of year to live in another region or climate. For example, birds leave the Arctic when temperatures drop in the fall, because the insects they feed on die.

molt In birds or mammals, to shed old feathers or a coat in order to grow a new covering.

North Pole The Earth's most northerly point.

permafrost Frozen ground in Arctic regions that never thaws.

predator An animal that hunts and eats other animals.

prey An animal that is hunted as food by a predator.

reindeer see **caribou**

rotate To turn on an axis. The Earth rotates once in about 24 hours.

South Pole The Earth's most southerly point.

tundra The vast area in the Arctic region of North America, Europe, and Asia where the subsoil never thaws.

Snowy owl

31

Index